(1/21)

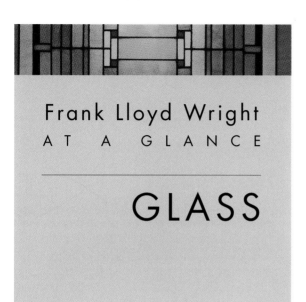

Frank Lloyd Wright
AT A GLANCE

GLASS

Frank Lloyd Wright
AT A GLANCE

GLASS

Doreen Ehrlich

B.T. Batsford Ltd • London

First published in 2001 by
B.T. Batsford Ltd,
8–10 Blenheim Court, Brewery Road, London N7 9NY

A member of the Chrysalis Group plc

© 2001 PRC Publishing Ltd.

ISBN 0 7134 8743 7

Printed and bound in China

Page iii: Detail of art glass from the Frank Lloyd Wright Home
and Studio, Oak Park, Chicago.

ACKNOWLEDGMENTS

The publisher wishes to thank Simon Clay for taking all the photography in this
book, including the cover photography, with the following exceptions:

Pages 33 and 35 © Alan Weintraub/Arcaid;
Page 81 (both) © Steelcase, Inc.;
The photograph on page 82 appears courtesy of The Metropolitan Museum of
Art, Purchase, Edgar J Kaufmann Foundation and Edward C Moore, Jr. Gifts,
1967 (67.231.1-.3). Photograph © 1978 The Metropolitan Museum of Art;
Page 84 (both) courtesy of John H Caulfield;
Back cover (top) © Bettmann/Corbis.

CONTENTS

INTRODUCTION

Glass is the material which, above all others, defines the work of Frank Lloyd Wright, from the use of art glass in his earliest houses in the first decade of the twentieth century to the dome of his last great commission, the Solomon R. Guggenheim Museum some sixty years later.

Throughout his long career, Wright was conscious of the importance of the material in his work. Writing in *The Architectural Record*, in 1928, Wright referred his audience to the unique properties of glass:

> "As a material we may regard it as a crystal-thin sheet of air in air to keep air out or
> keep it in and with this sense of it, we can think of uses to which it might be put as
> various and beautiful as the frost designs upon the pane of glass itself."

More pragmatic in practice than such poetic passages of his theoretical writing would suggest, Wright used advances in glass technology in the achievement of one of his prime objectives for both private and public buildings, that of the "vista without, vista within:" the breaking down of the conventional "box" of room-spaces, of both opening up the flow of spaces between internal areas and dissolving the boundaries between the building and its surrounding context where appropriate. In public buildings, where it was occasionally crucial to create an inward-looking space, Wright used glass to achieve a flow of natural light, as in the top-lit spaces of Unity Temple or the Solomon R. Guggenheim Museum.

RIGHT: Frank Lloyd Wright Studio, Oak Park, Illinois. View of the interior of the drafting room, part of the studio addition made to the house in 1895. The drafting room is an octagonally roofed two-story structure, in which the top lighting of the skylight diffuses the natural light to provide a perfect working light for an architectural practice. It is the precursor of all such top-lit spaces in Wright's work, from the Johnson Wax Building to the Guggenheim Museum.

YE'VE LEFT A GLIMMER STILL TO CHEER
THE MAN - THE ARTIFEX
THAT HOLDS IN SPITE O'KNOCKS AND SCALE
O'FRICTION WASTE AN' SLIP
AN' BY THAT LIGHT - NOW MARK MY WORD -
WE'LL BUILD THE PERFECT SHIP

Wright's earliest use of glass in domestic architecture was naturalistic in the stylized forms it employed, often using leaf and plant forms with occasional contrasting textures of frosted and clear glass. In his glass designs as elsewhere in his early work, Wright owed a great deal to Louis Sullivan, with whom Wright trained from 1888 to 1893, and who imbued in him a philosophy of architecture that remained with Wright throughout his life.

Wright left Sullivan and Adler's office in 1893, the year of the World's Columbian Exposition, which brought twenty-seven million visitors to the "White City" in Chicago over the summer. In the midst of an unprecedented building boom, Wright was part of a circle at the forefront of the city's development and his clients included such self-made men as the inventor William Wilmslow, who devised a process of electroglazing that was to become part and parcel of Wright's early art glass designs, which were innovative, brilliant, and widely copied. Wright explained the theory and practice of his designs in 1908, in "In the Cause of Architecture" thus: "The windows usually are provided with characteristic straight line patterns, absolutely in the flat and usually severe. The nature of the glass is taken into account in these designs as is also the metal bar used in their construction, and most of them are treated as metal 'grilles' with glass inserted forming a simple rhythmic arrangement of straight lines and squares made as cunning as possible so long as the result is quiet."

Electroglazing achieved such "quiet" results by utilizing straight zinc cames to hold the glass rather than the more customary lead cames that were broader, thicker, and more curvilinear. The staining of the glass too was "quiet." Wright preferred sharp, clear colors to enhance his abstracted forms, rather than the darker, more naturalistic palette favored by such contemporaries as Tiffany.

During the next six years of independent practice at Oak Park, the designs that emanated from Wright's studio were to transform domestic design and create new models for living both in the United States and, in the development of these new designs for what were to be termed "Prairie Houses," to a worldwide market far beyond the suburbs of Chicago through their publication in magazines and journals. Much of the success of these early designs lay in their "exotic" use of space and light, the "breaking of the box" and to their sympathetic use of natural materials which was in such strict contrast to the constraints of the general run of domestic architecture of the time. Especially remarkable was Wright's treatment of the windows, or fenestration, of the building. He particularly detested traditionally double-hung windows, terming these "guillotine" windows, and the way in which the light coming through such windows could only be seen as coming through a hole in the wall, rather than as a band of light—an extension of the room space and its relation to the exterior world.

The generously glazed areas of the Prairie designs were intimately related to their sites, but when, as with many of the early houses, they were situated on unprepossessing suburban sites, it was the "vista within" that became all-important. The most elaborate and, it could be argued, the finest of all the early commissions, the house built for Susan Lawrence Dana is a case in point. The inward-looking quality of its design and the richness of its glass ornamentation in particular compensates for the lack of natural vegetation of its site and draws in characteristic local natural forms as "organic" ornament.

Glass also plays a vital part in the greatest public commission of Wright's Chicago years. Unity Temple, designed in 1905 and dedicated in 1908, is a key building both in Wright's career and in the history of architecture. Wright responded to the exigencies of the noisy main street Oak Park site and the needs of the 400-strong congregation with what he termed "a noble room for worship...let that sense of the great room shape the whole edifice."

A year later, in 1909, Wright felt that he had reached an impasse in his life and work and he responded to an earlier invitation to go to Europe to assist in the publication of his designs in the highly influential *Wasmuth Portfolio*. On his return a year later he began to work on designs for a home which began life as a house for his mother, Anna Lloyd Wright, on a site where he had spent his childhood. Up until this time, all Wright's commissions had been for urban or suburban sites. Here at the first Taliesin, the building could be designed to take full advantage of the spectacular surrounding countryside and to take its place organically within it "a broad shelter" in Wright's words "seeking fellowship with its surroundings." At Taliesin the windows became long, uninterrupted bands of glass, protected by steep eaves, which enabled the windows to be left open "to the breezes of summer and become like an open camp if need be." Taliesin was designed as a self-sufficient working community, which incorporated a farm and other functional buildings, stretching gradually across the hill. Eventually the complex was to incorporate some 3,000 acres.

After the tragic fire and murders at Taliesin, in 1914, which resulted in the loss of his new family, Wright's life and work were never the same again. His work on the Imperial Hotel in Tokyo occupied him from 1916 to 1922 and he incorporated architectural elements, including the lighting of spaces and their relation to the outside world, of a culture he had long admired into his later work. The screen elements of his succeeding style are but one example of his life-long debt to Japanese design.

Subsequently, Wright's new clients in California required radically different solutions from their architect as did the sites and climactic conditions he was now called upon to work with. The four houses Wright built in the Los Angeles area while simultaneously working on the Aline Barnsdall ("Hollyhock House") and the Imperial Hotel commission were revolutionary both in their building technique and use of space and light. Wright used textured concrete block "the cheapest (and ugliest) thing in the building world," as he was to later describe it. The textile block construction, as Wright termed it, created its own spatial lexicon, taking its motif from the block itself. In an area of bright sunlight the textured wall blocks create shadows on the external elevations, a feature of the facades of each of the Barnsdall, Storer, Millard, Freeman, and Ennis residences.

Internally the textured block system provided Wright with hitherto undreamt of possibilities of manipulating light and shadow. The perforated blocks used at the Freeman House, for example, permit filtered light to create exciting shadow patterns in the interior spaces, while the raised living area of the two-story house has a series of clear windows which command superb views. The use of clear glass is in strict contrast to the textured concrete blocks with their stylized perforations which permit very little transmission of light. Identical blocks, lit from within, provided dramatic emphases to the exterior elevations. Wright's use of an inexpensive and innovative modular building system was confined in its textile block form to these Californian houses, as it did not find favor elsewhere.

In different times, however, Wright, the quintessential American architect, was to remember the lessons learnt in California to provide a solution to the problem of low-cost housing for middle-income families with his invention of the Usonian house during the Depression years. The derivation of the term "Usonian" is mysterious, but undoubtedly derives from "USA," not the contemporary United States of America which Wright now in his seventies perceived about him, but more a utopian idea of the future. As ever, however modest the building, Wright wanted to integrate the structure and the site, and this is a marked feature of the various types of Usonian homes, however different. This is nowhere more apparent than in their plan and the organization of interior space, which reflects the seismic changes in family life since Wright built his own home at Oak Park in the 1890s and particularly the changing status of women. The lighting of the interior was also crucial and involved the use of cut-out wooden screens, reminiscent of the perforated blocks of the California houses.

Most striking of these is, perhaps, the abstract design of the clerestory windows of the Pope-Leighey residence in Falls Church, Virginia. Unlike the Californian houses, this is a modest dwelling, whose ornament comes from the use of materials: brick and wood-joinery in striking tones of Cherokee Red. The house, built in 1941, was flexible in form, and the cut-out shapes of the clerestory windows frame changing views of the surrounding trees.

ABOVE: View of central brick chimney and hearth and the triple row of clerestory windows that provide top lighting throughout the central octagon at the Herbert F. Johnson Residence, "Wingspread," Wind Point, Wisconsin.

The Johnson & Son complex of buildings at Racine, Wisconsin was Wright's major public commission of the time. The administrative offices of 1936–39 and research laboratories (1944–50) demonstrated Wright's skill in devising inward-looking spaces in the use of the reverse-tapered columns of the main office and entrance lobby, where daylight is diffused through rows of pyrex glass tubes, shutting off the outside world. This created a paradoxical construction: one built by progressive methods to produce an internalized working environment reminiscent of the industrial ideals of the nineteenth century. The most startling use of glass in the building may be seen in the tunnel vaulted pedestrian bridge and the twenty-five-foot diameter of the reception area of the publicity department. Wright employed circular glass tubes made by Pyrex, which achieved his purpose of diffusing natural light and providing insulation while at the same time being self-supporting. In addition, the tubed windows provided elegant decorative opportunities while achieving their major function of refracting and diffusing light and cutting out the outside world.

Wright received some sixty commissions in the years between 1949 and 1959, proof, if proof were needed of his eminence in his last years. There was no end to his designing vitality: his last years were occupied both with an extraordinary range of building-types abroad, and, more significantly with prestigious public commissions across America, from the Marin Country Civic Center, in San Rafael, California, of 1962, to the Solomon R. Guggenheim Museum (1959), New York. Each was completed after Wright's death, and each might be said to employ devices taken from Roman architecture, particularly in their use of lighting.

The Marin County Civic Center in San Rafael, the largest structure designed by Wright demonstrates his continuing vitality and innovatory ideas to the last. So integrated is the vast complex to the spectacular landscape that deer graze in its immediate vicinity, proof of Wright's assertion that "when organic architecture is properly carried out no landscape is ever outraged by it, but is always developed by it."

Famously, Wright, when asked, "what is your masterpiece, your greatest work?" would reply "the next one." Now, however, over forty years after his death, it would seem unarguable that, especially after the recent restoration program, the crown of Wright's achievement, particularly in terms of his life-long concept of organic architecture, is the Solomon Guggenheim Museum, in New York.

The unique form and atmosphere of the great spiral ramp of the Guggenheim, which determines the visitor's progress through the museum is lit by a continuous band of skylights, a form familiar from Wright's earliest work. The radical glass tube technology used in the Johnson Wax Building was developed in the evolving design for the original "Modern Gallery" of 1945 for the skylights or "rifts" which ran the entire length of the ramp on its outer edge.

Wright conceived the monumental hemispherical dome, throughout the sixteen-year struggle it took him to realize the building he had intended, as the key to the whole "skyward" expansion of the great central space to what he termed the "flood of sunlight, illuminating the grand ramp." This crowning "oculus" or eye, and the natural light streaming from it, forms a fitting climax to Wright's conception of glass as "a crystal-thin sheet of air in air to keep air out or keep it in…we can think of uses to which it might be put as various and beautiful as the frost designs upon the pane of glass itself."

2

CASE STUDIES

FRANK LLOYD WRIGHT HOME AND STUDIO

Constructed: 1889–1906
Address: 951 Chicago Avenue, Oak Park, IL 60302.
Tours daily.

At the age of twenty-two, in 1889, Frank Lloyd Wright began to build a home for his wife and growing family with a loan of $5,000 from his employer and architectural mentor, Louis Sullivan. Originally a modest six-room bungalow, the house was added to over the course of two decades to become both a family home for his wife and six children and Wright's working environment with the later addition of a sizable studio containing a drafting room, an office, and a library.

The glass in much of the earlier part of the house is of a simple, geometric design, characteristic of Wright's work of the period. This can be seen in the lotus-like forms of the dining room glass, for example, and the more rectilinear forms of the windows of the barrel-vaulted children's playroom added to the house in 1895. The lotus-shaped glass of the dining room windows is framed by pale art glass, forming a minimal barrier between the house and the natural environment outside.

Such designs are also early evidence of Wright's dislike of figurative motifs for glass such as those used by his contemporary, Louis Comfort Tiffany, whose company, the Tiffany Glass and Decorating Company had established an international reputation by 1893, with the installation of a chapel at the World's Columbian Exhibition in Chicago. Wright's views were later expressed in characteristic fashion in "In the Cause of Architecture:" "Nothing is more annoying to me than any tendency of realism of form in window-glass, to get mixed up with the view outside. A window pattern should stay severely "put.""

RIGHT: Art glass illuminated ceiling grille above the dining room table. The forms of the design are curvilinear, set in a recessed wooden fretwork frame, which was illuminated to give the effect of light filtering through leaves. This was almost certainly the first of such devices in Wright's work, and electrically illuminated top lighting was to form an important feature of his later work.

In both the dining room and the children's playroom, the severity of the window glass design is offset by the extraordinary treatment of the top-lighting in each case. The barrel-vaulted playroom, which occupies the entire second floor of the new wing is fifteen feet high and is lit by an art-glass skylight set in a wooden fretwork screen in the ceiling and by windows that are treated as a near-continuous band of light. The windows are set at child-height, while adults must stoop to look out of them, an imaginative concept on Wright's part that extends to other features of the room such as the stair-stepped balcony, scaled for children, and the splendid mural that took its theme from *The Arabian Nights*. The lower windows have a rectilinear pattern that resembles a grid-like café curtain. A similar rectilinear pattern may be seen in the art-glass doors of the toy cabinets that flank the fireplace.

Whereas the dining room windows are set with a simple, geometric form of art glass in a cell-like design, placed high to ensure privacy and light diffusion, the ceiling is lit from above through a fretwork screen of amber and gold art glass that mirrors the shape of the dining table beneath it. The forms of the design are circular, set in a recessed grille, which at night glows to give the effect of light filtering through leaves. Such light screens were to form an important feature of Wright's work throughout his career.

ABOVE RIGHT: Dining room, showing ceiling grille and the simple geometric forms of the caming of the windows. The simplicity of the cell-like design of the windows, which are set high with sufficient patterning to ensure privacy and light diffusion may be contrasted to the circular forms of the amber and gold art glass illuminated fretwork ceiling grille, intended to give the effect of light filtering through leaves.

RIGHT: Studio window triptych. Wright's own studio contains the most spectacular and advanced glass in the whole home and studio complex. The three windows form the focal point of the room, focusing the view through the clear plate glass of the center of the triptych of windows.

LEFT: View of the interior of the children's playroom which occupies the entire second floor of the house. This was one of the additions made to the house in 1895 to accommodate Wright's growing family. The barrel-vaulted playroom is fifteen feet high and is lit by an art-glass skylight set in a wooden fretwork screen in the ceiling and by windows, set at child height, that are treated as a near continuous band of light.

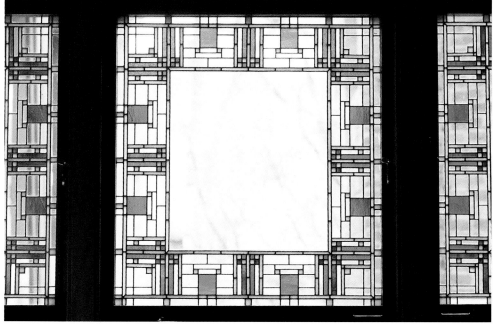

By 1895, with the proceeds from his work with the Luxfer Prism Company, Wright decided to run his growing architectural practice from home and began designing a display-piece studio addition to the house. The studio has a grand and complex separate entrance-way for clients who were given presentations in an impressive reception room. The complex of rooms demonstrate the radical development in Wright's thinking about the use of art glass, which had accelerated rapidly in a short space of time, forming a marked contrast to the less experimental glass seen in buildings designed for clients of the same period, and, indeed to the designs used in the family part of the building.

The drafting room is an octagonally roofed two-story structure, and the top lighting of the skylight diffuses the natural light to provide a perfect working light for an architectural practice. Wright's own studio also has a skylight and here the light is diffused through colored panels. It is in Wright's own working space that the most spectacular art glass in the studio complex, indeed in the whole ensemble of rooms, is to be found. The triptych of windows before Wright as he worked is formed of bright green and amber glass in a design constructed of squares, rectangles and bars. The view from the central window is thus framed in a manner that perfectly exemplifies Wright's dictum that "a window pattern should stay severely put" and "not get mixed up with the view outside."

Top lighting throughout the studio complex can be seen to be used for different purposes. For example, the three intricate art glass skylights of the studio reception room, in which clients and contractors were received, is not simply an integrated decorative feature but also serves the purpose of linking the drafting room, Wright's office, and the library. Light is diffused through the gold, sage, and amber art glass, whose patterns are interspersed with the occasional clear glass form. The tapestry-like forms of the glass at one and the same time diffuse light, as well as refracting it during the day, and also form what might be regarded as three framed glass abstract "pictures" in the ceiling, set as if they are in recessed wooden-framed panels.

The spectacular geometric art-glass designs of the skylights of the studio reception room and Wright's own study complex are in the greatest possible contrast to the curvilinear design of such elements as the ceiling grille above the dining room table in the adjacent house, where the amber and gold glass and curvilinear forms are intended to give the effect of light filtering through leaves and create a mood appropriate to the function of the room.

RIGHT: The studio skylight. One of the grandest and most dramatic of Wright's art-glass skylights, this design uses similar colors and squared and rectilinear forms to those employed in the studio window triptych, yet used in a different configuration appropriate to its purpose and to the fact that it is viewed from below, forming what might be regarded as a framed glass abstract "picture" in the ceiling, set as it is in deeply recessed wooden framed panels.

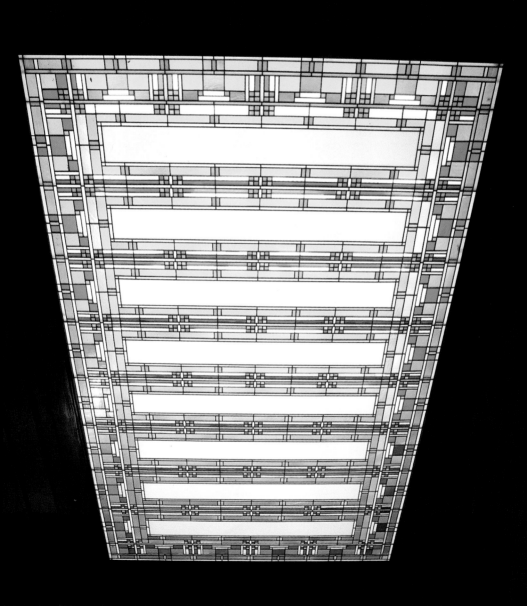

GEORGE BLOSSOM HOUSE

Constructed: 1892
Address: 4858 Kenwood Avenue, Chicago, IL 60615.

The George Blossom House of 1892 is one of several "bootleg" commissions designed while the young Wright was working for the partnership of Louis Sullivan and Dankmar Adler, who under the terms of his contract, expected the young architect to devote his time exclusively to them. When it became clear that the twenty-five year old apprentice had been working out of hours on such houses as the Blossom residence, Wright's tenure with the practice was summarily terminated. The Blossom residence is Colonial-Revival in form with a symmetrical front and clapboard siding in sharp contrast to the horizontal lines of the coach house, designed by Wright in 1907 on Prairie lines. The house itself is the most explicitly classical domestic design that Wright was to produce. A two-storied residence, like the contemporary design for the Charnley House, however traditional the exterior of the house the interior contains some highly original spaces and some fine early glass, designed by Wright to be in keeping with the austere lines of the building.

The glass designs show Sullivan's influence in the fanlight and flanking windows of the front entrance in their flowing curvilinear forms. However in the elegant dining room casements Wright used a square pattern that resembles the motifs employed in architecture of the Colonial period.

The casement windows of the dining room are set in a pattern of bordered squares forming a simple and striking design, which clearly and quintessentially exemplifies Wright's use of the casement window form, a form of fenestration which he valued above all others. Wright had a particular dislike of traditionally double-hung sash windows, terming these "guillotine" windows, deploring the fact that the way in which light

RIGHT: Detail of flanking windows of the entrance to the house. The shallow, curvilinear intersecting forms are characteristic of this early phase of Wright's Oak Park years. The austere yet elegant symmetry of the design is complementary to the architecture of the house, the most explicitly classical in form that Wright was to build.

came through such windows could only be seen as coming through such windows could only be seen as coming through a hole in the wall, rather than his preferred mode as a band of light—an extension of the room space and its relation to the exterior world.

Vistas were central to Wright's philosophy of architecture. The idea of casements opening onto the outside world required a radical rethinking of the traditional casement which opened onto the inward space, rather than, as with the dining-room windows of the Blossom residence, opening outward. This was such a radical departure from previous practice that many of Wright's early clients declined to proceed with commissions once the implications of the scheme were realized. Fortunately George Blossom had enough confidence in his young architect to allow him his way and the dining room window ensemble together with the elegant curvilinear designs of the entrance windows are witness to Wright's growing confidence as a designer, while remaining mindful of his mentor Sullivan's teaching that all ornament should be integral, utilising geometric forms drawn from nature.

RIGHT: Entry fanlight and flanking windows, seen against the light. The entrance windows of the Blossom House exemplify in their curvilinear forms and elegant symmetry the quality of repose sought by Wright in the design of domestic interiors from the very beginning of his career. Clients such as George Blossom required that their homes be all that their workplaces were not, a place apart, the "house beautiful," an ideal of domestic life that was current in both America and Europe at the time.

RIGHT, BELOW (LEFT): Detail of one of the flanking windows of the entrance to the house, showing the intersecting curvilinear forms so characteristic of Wright's work of the time, forms repeated in the arched skylight above the door and as variations on the abstract leaf-like forms in other glazed areas in the house.

RIGHT, BELOW (MIDDLE): The window design in the dining room (see detail to the right of this photograph) is witness to the young Wright's growing confidence as a designer, while remaining mindful of his mentor's teaching that all ornament should be integral, utilizing geometric forms drawn from nature.

RIGHT, BELOW (RIGHT): The casement windows of the dining room are set in an elegant pattern of bordered squares forming a simple and striking design which clearly exemplifies Wright's use of the casement window, a form of fenestration which he valued above all others. The idea of casement windows opening outward to the world required a radical rethinking of the traditional casement which opened onto the interior space.

LEFT: The Blossom House is the most explicitly classical domestic design that Wright was to produce with a symmetrical front and clapboard siding. The fine early glass designs are in keeping with the austere, elegant lines of the house as in the intersecting forms of this clear glass.

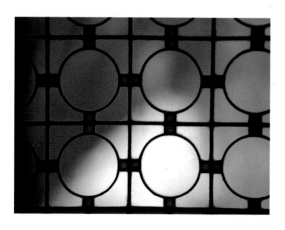

FRANK W. THOMAS HOUSE

Constructed: 1901
Address: 210 N. Forest Avenue, Oak Park, IL 60302.

The most remarkable of all Wright's early glass ensembles was perhaps that conducted in collaboration with the Italian designer Orlando Giannini of the glass stainers, Giannini and Hilgart (founded in 1899) at the residence of Frank Thomas at Oak Park in 1901. Wright's working partnership with Giannini and Hilgart, a successful collaboration between designer and makers that began early in the Oak Park period.

The entrance vestibule to the Thomas House (sometimes known as the "Harem") is particularly remarkable: Wright's conception of glass used as a continuous shimmering screen is realized in spectacular fashion. It amounts to an almost unbroken band of glass—his idea of an apparently continuous flow of space in which the walls seem to disappear is achieved in the form of a light-diffusing screen, which also helps insure privacy. Giannini and Hilgart's specialist skills are evident in the use of opalescent glass, gold leaf, and mother of pearl applied in varying degree to the stylized geometric forms.

A complex entryway is characteristic of many of Wright's houses of the period, few, however, are more complex than that of the Thomas House, which is reached by ascending two flights of stairs. The visitor is then made to change direction to discover the entrance door which is hidden from the street. Wright is thus controlling the visitor's reaction, encouraging them to experience the building's spatial dimensions before entering and setting up their expectation of what might await them once they gain the interior. The stylized

RIGHT: Entrance vestibule doors and windows seen against the light. The vestibule glass of the Frank W. Thomas House is innovative, creating a screen that ensures privacy while also diffusing the light.

forms of feathery wheat crown the design at the upper parts of the windows and doors of the vestibule, and the arrowhead designs and formalized ears of wheat that appear in the glass throughout the house are further elaborated in the golden skylight designs that appear almost as floating forms.

The Frank Thomas House, which may be regarded as Oak Park's first Prairie-style residence, is characterized, as are the other Prairie Houses, by its long, low, horizontal emphasis. The continuous bands of art glass help reinforce this horizontality, while the vertical lines of the arrowhead glass motifs help provide a necessary balance to the overall design. The use of such devices as mirrored gold leaf in the window detail reflects light and enhances the jewel-like effect of the windows, an effect that can be seen not merely by visitors to the house but by any passerby.

Wright's essay of 1928 "In the Cause of Architecture," might well be describing his own work at the Frank Thomas House of two decades before. He states that architectural glass should always be a "shimmering fabric woven of rich glass—patterned in color or stamped to form the metal tracery…to be in itself a thing of delicate beauty…expressing the nature of that construction in the mathematics of the structure."

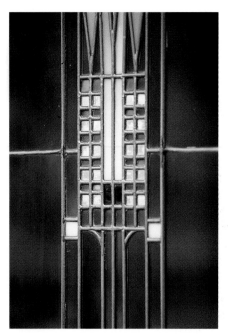

ABOVE RIGHT: Exterior elevation from the stair leading to the vestibule, showing art glass and original entrance light. A complex entryway is characteristic of many of Wright's houses of the period, few however are more complex than that of the Thomas House, which is reached by ascending two flights of stairs.

RIGHT AND LEFT: Details of art glass. Wright's working collaboration with the glass manufacturers Giannini & Hilgart includes the superb ensembles of glass that furnish the Frank W. Thomas House at Oak Park, one of the most elaborate of all Wright's art glass designs. The elegance of vertical lines of the arrowhead glass motifs and the jewel-like effect of the windows is enhanced by such devices as the use of opalescent glass and mirrored gold leaf applied in varying degree to the stylized geometric forms.

THE SUSAN LAWRENCE DANA (DANA–THOMAS) HOUSE

Constructed: 1902
Address: 301 E. Lawrence Avenue, Springfield, IL 62703.
Tours Wednesday through Sunday.

Wright was given almost free rein and a near unlimited budget by the wealthy socialite for a house in which to entertain her prestigious social and political circle on a lavish scale. The generous budget allowed Wright to employ the Linden Glass Company's expertize on a grand scale, with some 450 bespoke panels and 200 custom-made light fittings throughout the house.

The grand residence, completed in 1904, comprised thirty-five rooms of wonderful variety and intricacy. Throughout the house, the use of glass in the major social spaces is instrumental is creating a flow of light and opening up the interior. This begins with the entrance itself, where the function of the house as a suitable setting for a society and political hostess, and an important social focus for the area, may be read into the interlocking butterfly forms of the glass of the entrance arch, which may be intended to represent Susan Lawrence Dana's status as a social butterfly. Wright exploits the decorative possibilities of iridiscent glass in the splendid fanlight which appears green and blue in tone from outside and amber and pale gold against the light of the exterior.

The great barrel-vaulted space of the dining room is lit by clerestory windows, where Wright employs the prairie flower, the sumac, together with Fall tones seen throughout the house in a series of repeating motifs. The arched window below the vault also carries sumac designs, which offer subtle variations of color and form on the prevailing motifs in the same distinctive coloration.

RIGHT: Detail of the glass of the Fountain Doors. The stylized floral motifs of the doors and windows are related in design and are not entirely symmetrical, a device that adds variety to the visual experience. The use of iridiscent and opalescent glass is striking and the whole ensemble represents a tour de force of design and craftsmanship.

However splendid the glass elsewhere in the house, it was the art glass of the fountain doors and windows that the Linden Glass Company chose to exemplify their work in their advertisements. The ensemble comprises four windows and six doors, and here the motif is not that of the upright prairie sumac but pendant flowers resembling wisteria or, possibly, laburnum.

The windows of the studio form a marked contrast to the glass elsewhere in the house. The series of panels appear to be suspended from the caming of the upper registers of the window for which Wright coined the term "suspended glass screen" while the design employs plant-like abstractions unique in Wright's work.

The Dana House may fairly be typified as the most opulent, the best preserved, and most complete example of Wright's aesthetic of the Prairie years.

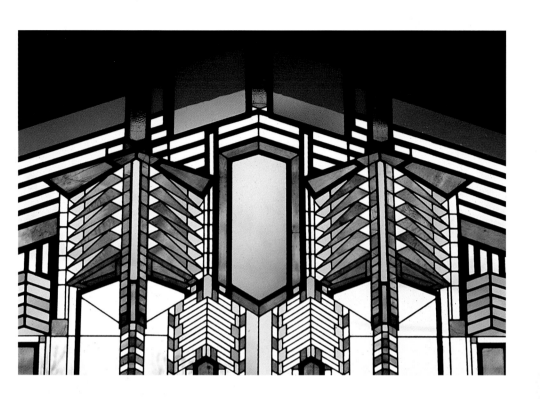

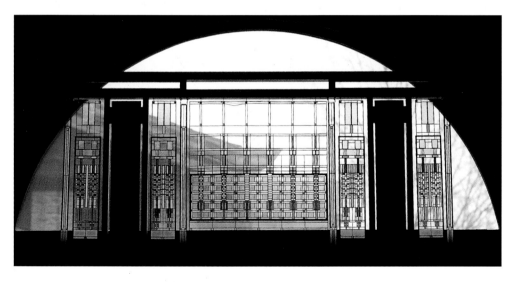

UNITY TEMPLE

Constructed: 1905
Address: 875 Lake Street, Oak Park, IL 60302
Guided and self guiding tours available.

Wright's major public building of his years in Oak Park was the Unity Temple, a major commission for the small studio in 1905, and one that was particularly exacting in its use of glass. The Unitarian-Universalist congregation had a modest budget of some $45,000, and this necessitated the use of economic building materials. The solid masonry of reinforced concrete decided upon was turned to brilliant effect both in the aesthetics of the design and the practical need for a peaceful space on what was then a heavily trafficked site.

Wright himself saw Unity Temple as a watershed in his career. Interviewed some fifty years after it was built, he reflected "I think that was about the first time when the interior space began to come through as the reality of that building. When you sat in Unity Temple, you were sitting under a big concrete slab but your eyes go out into the clouds on four sides. There were no walls with holes in them." Today, nearly a hundred years later, on entering the building the visitor is made aware of the continuity between the outside world and the inner sanctum of the temple by the use of Wright's characteristic "light screens," which here take the form of art glass windows and doors. Wright termed the temple his "jewel box," for reasons made clear when entrance is made through the dark cloister into the interior. The eye is led directly to the magnificent coffered

RIGHT: Daylight filters through the amber ceiling glass, creating the feel of a warm summer day below, whatever the time of year.

skylights, which form the entire ceiling. Of amber and beige glass and in a pattern of squares and rectangles, each is set at a different angle to the whole.

Wright conceived the Temple as a cube, "a noble form of masonry." The overhead structure is carried on four hollow concrete posts, which enables the walls to be non-supporting and to act as screens, an effect further enhanced by the band of light screens immediately below the roof, forming a clerestory, or "clearstory," as in a medieval cathedral. Wright's use of art glass in the top lighting and in the side alcoves was intended, as he himself wrote "to get a sense of a happy cloudless day into the room... daylight sifting through between the intersecting concrete beams, filtering through amber glass ceiling lights. Thus managed, the light would, rain or shine, have the warmth of sunlight."

The simple, yet powerful geometry of the spatial design is further integrated by the use of solid spheres, squares, and cubes in the design of the light fittings, and the golden and amber tones of the whole extend to the minute and painstaking detail of the gold silk that covers the wiring of the lamp fixtures. Unity Temple has undergone major restoration in recent years and is now resplendent in its detail.

RIGHT: Wright's use of light in the Unity Temple includes a band of light screens providing top-lighting as well as beautifully designed artificial light fixtures.

LEFT: The continuous band of windows or light screens immediately beneath the translucent roof of the interior. This clerestory, together with Wright's use of art glass in the top lighting and the side alcoves was intended to replicate the feel of sunlight.

FREDERICK C. ROBIE HOUSE

Constructed: 1908
5757 S. Woodlawn Avenue, Chicago, IL 60637
Guided Tours available.

Built between 1908 and 1910, the Robie House is generally agreed to be the culmination of Wright's conception of the Prairie House. It is remarkable for its many refinements, not least in its adaptation to the extremes of climatic conditions in Chicago. In addition to the technological subtleties of the heating and ventilation, the refinement of the brick-built design can be seen from such features as the steeply pitched roof overhang, so designed as to provide maximum protection from the powerful Chicago sunlight. Even in the middle of summer the noon sun does not strike the south-facing dining room. Such control of the "the vista without," enables "the vista within" to be lit by an extraordinary series of windows that are markedly light and elegant in style.

The interior of the Robie House perfectly exemplifies Wright's concept of "every house worth considering as a work of art must have a grammar of its own…a great thing instead of a collection of smaller ones." His commission included designs for the oak furniture, carpeting, and light fixtures as well as the glass throughout the house. Both motifs and color tonalities are drawn from the presiding "grammar" of the dominant geometric designs which prevail throughout the house. Linked motifs appear in the carpet designs and in the window glass and these two-dimensional forms are echoed in the three-dimensional forms of the furniture to produce an extraordinarily integrated whole.

RIGHT: View of the dining area windows. The same pattern is used in the glass of both windows and doors of the entire main living space, giving the effect of dissolving the wall into shimmering light while retaining a sense of enclosure. The pattern utilizes diagonal forms and flattened diamond shapes that are echoed in the three dimensional forms of the oak furniture.

The geometric motifs of the glass do not appear to have a direct basis in any plant form but would seem to be angular abstractions. However when used in their fullest form—as in the splendid ranked row of art glass windows of the living room—it is apparent that the angular forms are combined with grain shafts, in a symbolic reference to the prairie, while the design of the carpet motifs is a segment of a related form. The verticality and angularity of the glass motifs serve both to stress and counterbalance the horizontality of the design of the house as a whole.

Wright's view, expressed in 1928, that "pattern is made more cheaply and beautifully effective when introduced into the glass of the windows than in the use of any other medium that architecture has to offer" is nowhere more readily perceived than in the Robie House, where the clear flow of the spaces as a whole and the general lightness and elegance of the ambience of the rooms is enhanced by the delicate counterpoint of the glass motifs.

ABOVE RIGHT: View of living room seating area, showing the complex integration of motifs and color tonalities used throughout the house. The geometric motifs of some of the forms in the the glass, which resemble grain shafts, can be viewed as a symbolic reference to the prairie.

RIGHT: View of living room area showing the complementary motifs in the window glass, lighting fixtures, and built-in furniture.

LEFT: View of the main living area toward the hearth, which provides the only separation between living and dining areas. Regarded as the culmination of Wright's conception of the Prairie House, the house is remarkable for its many refinements, not least in the integrated "grammar" of its decorative forms.

ALINE BARNSDALL HOUSE
"HOLLYHOCK HOUSE"

Constructed: 1917
Address: Barnsdall Art Park, 4808 Hollywood Boulevard, Los Angeles, CA 90027.
House closed for renovation.

Wright called the house he designed for the heiress Aline Barnsdall, the first of his "California Romanza," a term that refers to his distinctively romantic interpretation of the site and its cultural antecedents as well as the requirements of his client. Wright conceived this and the other houses in the area as "dream houses," realizations of a fantasy which draw on the particular spirit of the place. In the case of the Barnsdall House, Wright's inspirational interpretation related to pre-Columbian culture—the motifs of the house are reminiscent of Mayan temple structures, although they are freely interpreted in Wright's inimitable manner. Hollyhock motifs are present throughout the design, both in the structure and the furniture and fittings, and the distinctive art glass employs stylized triangular forms of the flower. Wright's work on the Imperial Hotel, Tokyo, may also be seen as an influence, not only in the splendid Japanese artworks that adorn the house, but in such features as the skylights (as can be seen in the living room), which are of a form he was currently using in the Tokyo design. The living room skylight is formed of a rectilinear wooden frame interspersed with long lines of tiny geometric patterned glass and clear glass, which give a lightness of feeling and structure new to Wright's work.

The use of art glass throughout the house, and in the nursery and living quarters designed for Aline Barnsdall's small daughter, is distinctive and includes the use of diagonal features and an overall "busyness" of form, that would suggest unusual intervention on the part of the client whose brief included an ampitheater and a performance space incorporated in the entrance loggia. Wright's distinctive use of glass is seen at its most characteristic in the low-ceilinged space of the child's playroom, with its walls of art glass in diagonal

RIGHT: Detail of playporch windows. The use of art glass throughout the nursery and living quarters designed for Aline Barnsdall's small daughter is distinctive. The low-ceilinged space has walls of art glass in diagonal forms in purple tones.

patterns and triangular forms in purple tones, a coloration unusual in Wright's work. This must have been an enchanting space for a child: designing for children appears to have evoked a special response in Wright, as is obvious from the design of the playroom for his own six children in the house at Oak Park and the Coonley Playhouse windows.

Elsewhere in the house the glass is similarly distinctive; the dining room windows, for example, employ diagonal forms that echo the motifs of the imposing dining room suite, a tour de force of stylized hollyhocks. The master bedroom also boasts some fine glass, here a sequence of five floor-to-ceiling windows, flanked by two further windows, which command superb views of the landscaping of Olive Hill.

Wright employed the architect Rudolph Schindler, newly arrived in America to oversee construction on the site in his absence in Tokyo. Schindler's comment on the windows of the playroom might also stand for other windows in the house, such as those of the bedroom: "They are not wall holes, but a dissolution of the building material into a grid—eaded glass—as the ground dissolves and becomes lost in the tree branches."

ABOVE RIGHT: Art glass windows of the master bedroom. This splendid run of windows, a sequence of five floor-to-ceiling windows, flanked by two further windows, commands superb views of Olive Hill. The abstracted flower design and pallette drawn from the hollyhock motif seen throughout the house is here used in a more open fashion as the glass screen is on an upper floor.

RIGHT: Playporch window and door showing the diagonal motifs of abstract hollyhock forms. Aline Barnsdall's daughter "Sugartop" (Aline Elizabeth) had her own suite of rooms, including this low-ceilinged playroom.

LEFT: Detail of the exterior showing the distinctive abstracted hollyhock design that runs throughout the house. Here it is seen in the textured concrete block column and in the glass.

MABEL AND CHARLES ENNIS HOUSE (ENNIS–BROWN HOUSE)

Constructed: 1923–24
Address: 2607 Glendower Avenue, Los Angeles, CA 90027-1114.
Special tours available by reservation to Friends of the Ennis–Brown House
at the above address.

The Mabel and Charles Ennis House was the last house by Wright to incorporate art glass. Designed in 1923, it is the grandest and most monumental of all the concrete textile block houses, and the last of the genre. Conspicuous on its ridge in the Santa Monica Mountains, the house is in fact smaller than it appears. Wright had always sought dramatic sites, which heightened in his words "the true property of character." The drama inherent in the site is reflected in the architecture, for which Wright used a form of stacked textile block, patterned with forms reminiscent of Mayan motifs, although the design is one of the most eclectic and fantastic of all Wright's works. As one of the futuristic settings for Ridley Scott's *Bladerunner* (1989–1991) it achieved iconic status in the collective memory six decades after it was built.

Wright's final use of art glass is as spectacular as the building and the site it commands, moreover there are links with his earliest commissions in Illinois. He may well have employed the talents of his trusted glass maker of the Oak Park years, Orlando Giannini, who is known to have been living in La Jolla at the same time as Wright during the period in which the house was constructed. The abstract motifs in the glass—notably that of the living room, in the smaller dining room windows, and in the library doors and windows—may be seen as partially derived from plant forms indigenous to the area, as with the early art glass of such houses as the Susan Lawrence Dana Residence.

RIGHT: Detail of window glass showing abstract forms derived from plant forms indigenous to the area, as with the early art glass in such buildings as the Dana Thomas House. Although employing a different pallette, the subtleties of color in the glass are also reminiscent of the early glass, and this may point to the collaboration of Wright's trusted glass maker of the Oak Park years, Orlando Giannini, who was then working in the Los Angeles area.

The main dining room window commands a spectacular view of Los Angeles, framed in a triptych form, familiar from Wright's early work. The diagonal forms incorporated into the design are reminiscent of those used in the Barnsdall House, but these are pure abstractions, with a symmetry, harmony, and balance that might be termed classical. The caming is delicate with subtle variations of width, and the scintillating points of color of the tiny glass fragments are set in satisfying counterpoint against the clear panes.

Another link with Wright's early work is to be seen in the spectacular glass overmantel of the colonnade, which would appear to be from Giannini's workshop, as it is reminiscent in its wisteria design of the mantels of both the Darwin D. Martin House and the Husser House in Chicago, designed by Blanche Ostertag and made by Giannini. Both are now lost and the survival of the Ennis House mantel marks a fitting culmination of Wright's most fruitful working partnership, all the more remarkable given the fact that the house has suffered much from earthquake damage and the imperfections inherent in the textile block process.

ABOVE RIGHT: Detail of bathroom windows. The Ennis–Brown House was the last house designed by Wright to incorporate art glass as well as being the grandest and most monumental of all the textile block houses, and the last of the genre. The attention to detail throughout the house is exemplified by the windows of the bathroom in which the scintillating points of color in a pallette seen throughout the house are here set against textured glass panes to form a privacy screen.

RIGHT: Window triptych of the main dining room. The main window commands a spectacular view, framed in a triptych form, familiar from Wright's early work.

LEFT: Detail of window glass showing the subtle variations of width in the caming and the tiny fragments of art glass which form scintillating points of color against the clear panes. The contrast between the extreme delicacy of the glass design and the concrete textile blocks that form the house is markedly complementary.

THE SAMUEL FREEMAN HOUSE

Constructed: 1923–24
Address: 1962 Glencoe Way, Hollywood, CA 90068
The house is closed for restoration.

The small house built for Samuel and Harriet Freeman was the last of Frank Lloyd Wright's West Coast concrete textile block residences. The compact house is built on a steep site, so designed that it and its terraces appear to be perfectly integrated into the hillside. The interior of the house is designed to provide both the idea of shelter and the vista within, so central to Wright's domestic dwellings and to maximize the "vista without" as it is so oriented that the main living room windows command spectacular views of Los Angeles.

Glass is used in fantastic and imaginative fashion throughout the house. The house is formed of sixteen-inch concrete blocks, some of which are embellished with a distinctive geometric flower design, and identical blocks are perforated and glazed to form light-filtering units. Strong sunlight shining through the perforations forms distinctive patterns of light and shadows in the interior spaces, adding to the cave-like atmosphere of the main living space and contributing to the extraordinary design of the whole structure.

RIGHT: View of the living room. The space is lit by both perforated and glazed blocks in the same flower design that is used throughout the structure on the main level and by clerestory windows of the same pattern. The patterned and perforated blocks flank a large picture window to the terrace with spectacular views of Los Angeles and beyond.

The glazed and perforated blocks are set in counterpoint to the extensive areas of glazing, where the mullions of the windows exactly mirror the lines of the concrete blocks, forming a new and exciting variant on a quintessential Wrightian design element, that of the glass screen. The corners of the building are particularly distinctive as the glass appears to continue around the building thus literally "breaking the box," and contributing to the apparent lightness of the design and belying the weight and density of the concrete.

The living room space is lit by both perforated blocks on the main level and by clerestory windows above. Both have the same pattern, forming light and shadow designs of extraordinary variety at different

times of day. The patterned and perforated blocks flank a large picture window to the terrace with superb views of Los Angeles below, and beyond to the distant horizon.

LEFT: Detail of the facade showing the distinctive concrete blocks which form the house, some of which are perforated and glazed to filter light. The blocks are set against the glazed areas, which appear to continue around the building thus contributing to the apparent lightness of the design.

RIGHT: View of the facade showing the glazed and perforated blocks set in counterpoint to the extensive areas of glazing, where the mullions of the windows exactly mirror the lines of the sixteen-inch concrete blocks. The corners of the building are particular distinctive as the glass appears to become invisible, with panes butted against each other without a corner mullion, thus appearing to literally achieve Wright's constant aim of "breaking the box."

S.C.JOHNSON WAX ADMINISTRATION BUILDING

Constructed: 1936
Address: Golden Rondell Theater, 1525 Howe Street, Racine, WI 53403.
Guided tours available by reservation.

Wright conceived the design of the Administration Building as an inward-looking "sealed space," in which the radical use of glass tube walls made it impossible for the workers to see the outside world, and the industrial activity which surrounded it. In its solution to a complex problem, the building is reminiscent of Wright's early work of 1904, the Larkin Administration Building, which had been dedicated to what the architect described as the "unpopular gospel of work," although the sheer concrete walls and toplighting of the Larkin Building are replaced with walls of light. In *The Autobiography*, Wright wrote of the Johnson complex, "Organic architecture designed this great building to be as inspiring a place to work as any cathedral ever was in which to worship," and the analogy is made clearer both by the height of the building and in its use of glass to flood the interior.

The administrative office of 1936–39 demonstrated Wright's skill in devising inward-looking spaces most effectively, perhaps in the spaces of the central workroom where daylight is diffused through rows of pyrex glass tubes providing a filtered sunlit interior, in a space which effectively shuts off the outside world to the workers within it as it is impossible to see through the tubed glass screens which both refract and diffuse the light. The effect is further enhanced by the graceful concrete columns of the interior which are reminiscent of huge lily pads. The tunnel vaulted pedestrian bridge and the twenty-five foot diameter of the reception area of the publicity department are formed of walls and ceilings of circular glass tubes made by pyrex, which achieve Wright's purpose of diffusing natural light and providing insulation, at the same time being self-supporting. In addition, the tubed windows provided elegant and minimalistic decorative opportunities. The only drawback to the use of such technology lay in the manner in which the

RIGHT: Interior view of the tunnel vaulted pedestrian bridge linking the publicity department and the executive department. Lumiline bulbs were inserted between two layers of glass tubing to illuminate the space by diffusing electric light, giving the appearance of translucent natural light at night, a revolutionary concept that demonstrates Wright's extraordinary power to innovate, even in his seventh decade.

tubes were prone to leaking before a clear silicone caulking process was invented. Wright himself had insisted that there were to be no windows in the building. The lighting is a revolutionary concept executed with a brilliance that shows Wright's extraordinary and continuing dynamism in his seventh decade. He is said to have desired that the environment for the workers in the building would be reminiscent of a glade with fresh air and sunshine all the time.

The Administrative Offices complex received the addition of a tower, housing the Research Laboratories, which was built between 1944 and 1950. The corners of the tower are rounded, in what has been described as aerodynamic fashion, and, as with the earlier building, the windows are formed of rows of glass tubes to diffuse the light. The effect of the entire complex from both the interior and exterior is streamlined and of the moment, bringing Wright back into the public eye with the sheer amount of publicity it provoked and rescuing the architect's flagging financial fortunes.

LEFT: Corner of the Research Tower, showing the streamline appearance so admired when it was first built. The tower housing the Research laboratories, was built between 1944 and 1950 and formed a striking addition to the complex. The corners of the tower are rounded, in what was described by contemporaries as aerodynamic fashion, and, as with the earlier building, the windows are formed of rows of glass tubes which gives the tower its characteristic streamlined effect.

ABOVE RIGHT: Interior view showing the curved glass walls of the entirely windowless interior, which achieve Wright's purpose of diffusing natural light and providing insulation while at the same time being self-supporting. The tubed walls provided both diffused and refracted light and cut out the world outside. Although their form follows their function, the tubed walls are elegant in their simplicity.

RIGHT: Detail of tubed screen wall, showing the joints of the circular Pyrex tubes. Lumiline bulbs were inserted between two layers of glass tubing to illuminate the building at night by diffusing electric light, simulating the effect of sunlight. The major drawback to the use of such technology lay in the manner in which the tubes were prone to leaking before a clear silicone caulking process was invented.

FAR RIGHT: Whilst the innovative use of the pyrex tubes enabled Wright to achieve his purpose of diffusing and refracting natural light as well as providing insulation, they were also elegant and minimalistic in their decorative manner and showed Wright's extraordinary and continuing dynamism even in his seventh decade.

a Innovative use of materials: the use of Pyrex tubes was radical at the time, diffusing and refracting the light as well as providing insulation. The walls were also self-supporting, and night-time illumination could be provided by Lumiline bulbs inserted between two layers of glass tubing.

b "Breaking the box:" one of Wright's abiding principles throughout his long career was the breaking down of the barriers between exterior and interior space and the creation of the "vistas within" and "vistas without." The dominant curved motifs of the interior vista are set against the clear glass of the entrance, through which may be seen the repeating concrete curves of the "vista without."

c Integrated design: the simple geometric curved forms of the walls are repeated in the furniture throughout the building, which was all designed by Wright himself. The dominant motif of the curve seen in the tubular construction of both chairs and walls is reflected in the design of the ceiling.

d Advanced technology: the joints in the glass proved problematic when the building was first constructed before a clear silicone caulking process was invented. It is said that even Mr Johnson's office was not immune from the leakage and that an empty trash can was kept near his desk to catch the drips when necessary.

HERBERT F. JOHNSON HOUSE "WINGSPREAD"

Constructed: 1937

Address: The Johnson Foundation, 333 East Four Mile Road, Wind Point, WI.

Tours available outside business hours.

"Wingspread" was built for Herbert F. "Hib" Johnson, grandson of the founder of Johnson's Wax, and its president. The Johnson's Wax headquarters building dates from 1936–39, and Wingspread, which was Wright's largest and most expensive domestic commission to date, was built at the same time. The principles inherent in its design were radically different from that of the Headquarter's complex, with much emphasis on craftsmanship and a unique employment of glass throughout the structure. As with other buildings by Wright, the qualities of Wingspread are related directly to the nature of the site, which partly determined its form. The site was barely half a mile from Lake Michigan, on a former nature reserve comprising some thirty acres of land that included a ravine and a lake. It would appear that Wright regarded Wingspread as a development of the Prairie House of half a century before, although the land it occupies is far more extensive than even that of the Avery Coonley house.

RIGHT: View of central octagon and clerestory windows from the hearth area. Wright considered Wingspread to be the best built and costliest house he had designed to date. There was much emphasis on craftsmanship and a unique employment of glass throughout the structure, which otherwise used red brick, cypress, and pink Kasota sandstone as its building materials.

The center of the pinwheel layout of the house is the monumental brick chimney that is the core of the building and a reworking of the principle of Wright's "sacred hearth" on a grand scale. Certain features of the use of glass in the design recall Wright's own house and studio at Oak Park at the very beginning of the century. This is particularly evident in the central octagon where clear glass panes afford dramatic top-lighting in a radical elaboration of the drafting room octagon. However, at Wingspread the octagon rises through three stories and is the light-filled core of the house from which all four wings radiate. Natural light falls through triple bands of clerestory windows and light decks onto the curvilinear form of the monumental central chimney at the heart of the octagon.

On three of its sides the octagon is further illuminated by French doors that rise through two stories, all of which employ the clear glass panes used throughout the house. The curvilinear forms of the brick chimney and the dramatic curved stair behind it that leads to the observation tower all act as counterpoint to the square grid on which the house is constructed. Such square forms run throughout the fenestration of the central space of Wingspread, creating a calm and harmonious living space unlike any other in Wright's work.

LEFT: View of central hearth area with seating, French windows and terrace beyond, and clerestory windows. The comfortable seating around the hearth is characteristic of the light-filled elegance of the design of Wingspread, where all such living and entertaining spaces are articulated around the central core of the great chimney, which has a hearth on each level.

ABOVE: View of clerestory windows, central chimney, and the circular staircase leading to the observation platform. The top-lighting of the great central space throws dramatic shadows, seen here falling on the upper register of the central chimney.

RIGHT: View up into clerestory from the hearth. According to Wright, Wingspread, built for Herbert F. Johnson, was the last of the Prairie Houses, albeit of a pinwheel design.

V.C. MORRIS GIFT SHOP

Constructed: 1948
Address: 140 Maiden Lane, San Francisco, CA 91408.
The gallery is open during normal business hours.

In 1948 Wright was to return to California after a space of thirty years. The projects achieved in his last decade spent there were very different from his earlier domestic commissions, the California Romanza, of the Aline Barndsdall "Hollyhock House," and the Mabel and Charles Ennis House. The monumental Marin County Civic Center, San Rafael, California is the major Californian project of his last decade and was completed after Wright's death. In contrast the tiny V.C. Morris Gift Shop in the center of San Francisco was begun in 1948 and completed within the year.

The dark, cave-like entrance to the shop gives no indication of what lies within, although, particularly at night, attention is subtly drawn to the arched opening by the horizontal and vertical lights set into the brickwork. The site of the shop is a narrow one, and Wright turns this to advantage by both accentuating the theatrical entrance arch which is reminiscent of a Roman tunnel vault and emphasizing the treatment of the fine brickwork of the facade with fine horizontal mortar joints. Thus the spectator is drawn to the facade, which is entirely windowless when it is seen from across the narrow street, and, on approaching, can admire the fine detail of the brickwork, which sets the shop apart from the surrounding buildings and has weathered particularly gracefully.

At the time it was built, the dramatic windowless facade of the V.C. Morris shop set it apart from retail design of the time, although such facades were to become a familiar feature of boutique design across the world a decade later. Postwar shop design was still based on the idea of the plate glass display windows

RIGHT: Interior view of the ramp, looking up into the top-lighting of the roof. The spiral form of the defining ramp of the interior, which extends through the two stories of the shop is echoed in the circular forms that abound elsewhere. The ramp is generally perceived to be a forerunner on a small scale of that of the Solomon R .Guggenheim Museum in New York.

used by Wright's mentor, Louis Sullivan, in the Carson Pirie Scott store in Chicago some fifty years before. The new technology at the beginning of the century which made possible such spectacular shop windows was designed to attract shoppers to the goods in the windows, whereas one has to enter the V.C. Morris store, or at least approach the tunnel-vaulted entrance to see what is inside.

Once inside the shop, it is possible to see why the interior is often perceived as a forerunner of the Guggenheim Museum on a small scale. The spiral form of the defining ramp of the interior, which extends through the two stories of the shop is echoed in the circular forms that abound elsewhere in the interior design. The visitor ascends the ramp to view the goods set out in the elegant interior from changing vantage points, while further goods are displayed in a series of display cases set into the concrete of the ramp. The subtle internal illumination of the display cases is enhanced by the extraordinarily sophisticated lighting of the entire interior. This is achieved by a characteristically Wrightian use of top-lighting diffused through the glass roof, which is further enhanced by a series of hemispherical light forms and a further series of recessed circular lights, which all contribute to the elegant, spacious ambience of the shop, belying its comparatively tiny space.

As with other Wright public buildings on busy city-center sites such as Unity Temple at the very beginning of his career and, most famously, the Guggenheim Museum to come, Wright turns the design in on

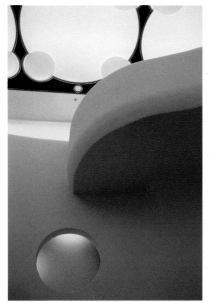

itself in order to create a calming and peaceful room removed from the bustle and stress of city life. The uniqueness of the building and the care lavished on the detail may be in part explained by Wright's friendship with V.C. Morris for whom he was also to design a house.

RIGHT: View of the exterior across Maiden Lane. The site of the shop (now a gallery) is an exceptionally narrow one and the dark, cave-like entrance of the windowless facade gives no indication of what lies within. Wright turns the site to advantage by emphasizing the entrance arch which is reminiscent of a Roman tunnel vault and accentuating the treatment of the brickwork of the facade with fine mortar joints. At night attention is subtly drawn to the shop by the horizontal and vertical lights set into the brickwork of the defining walls.

LEFT: Interior showing the ground floor, the ramp and the top-lighting which is diffused through the glass roof and further enhanced by a series of hemispherical light forms and a further series of recessed circular lights. The visitor ascends the ramp to view both goods and shop from changing vantage points, while further goods are displayed in a series of cases set into the concrete of the wall of the ramp.

THE SOLOMON R. GUGGENHEIM MUSEUM (1956)

Constructed: 1956
Address: 5th Avenue at 88th Street, New York, NY 10028-0173.
Museum hours, closed Thursdays and Christmas Day.

1959, the year of Wright's death at the age of ninety-two, finally saw the opening of the most significant and controversial buildings of his last decade. The commission for the museum had first been mooted in 1943 and a year later Wright defined his idea of a modern museum that placed particular stress on the light and space of the interior: "A museum should be one extended well-proportioned floor space from bottom to top—a wheelchair going around and up and down, throughout. No stops anywhere and such screened divisions of the space gloriously lit within from above as would deal appropriately with every group of paintings or individual paintings as you might want them classified." The spiral ramp, which takes five complete turns around the central void, determines the visitor's progress through the building and the gentle backward tilt of the sloping walls on which the paintings are placed are designed to replicate the angle of an artist's easel.

Wright believed that paintings were best experienced in the changing conditions of natural light, a truth to which most the great galleries of the world attest. Wright's solution to the problem of lighting the museum was intended to replicate natural light as far as possible, and to that end the radical glass-tube technology used in the Johnson Wax Building was developed in the design for the original skylights or "rifts," which ran the entire length of the internal ramp on its outer edge, enclosing a system of incandescent tubes, subtly enhancing the natural light that floods through the space from the monumental hemispherical dome, the key to the whole "skyward" expansion of the great central space.

The exterior of the Guggenheim is notoriously antithetical to its surroundings, while the ivory-painted interior creates its own tranquil world in opposition to its site. Wright elaborated on the paradox, likening the effect of the interior of the building to "that made by a still wave, never breaking, never offering resistance or finality to vision. It is this extraordinary quality of the complete repose known only in movement that characterizes this building."

The Guggenheim is created as a total environment, one that in Wright's words creates a "new unity between beholder, painting, and architecture."

RIGHT: The hemispherical dome and spiral ramp viewed from below. The light that floods the building from the monumental hemispherical dome was enhanced by the series of skylights or "rifts", enclosing a system of incandescent tubes, that replicate natural light as far as possible and offers the best environment for viewing works of art.

OVERLEAF: View from below of the central ramp. The radical glass tube technology used in the Johnson Wax building was developed in the design for the skylights or "rifts".

MARIN COUNTY CIVIC CENTER

Constructed: 1960

Address: San Rafael, California 3501 Civic Center Drive, San Rafael, CA 94903.

Open during business hours.

Wright received the commission for the huge Marin County Civic Center in 1957 and presented his plans just under a year later. A model was produced and only the working drawings remained to be finished at the time of Wright's death in 1959. Construction, by the Taliesin Fellowship, of the eight million dollar project was begun in February 1960. Thus the last building designed by Wright—and by far the largest—demonstrates that his radical response to challenge remained constant to the very end of his life. The monumental complex contains the county offices, the courts of justice, the central library, the jail, and other civic spaces. The two vast wings of the center are concrete built, and the circular and semi-circular modular forms have a distinctive presence, one that may be said to evoke Roman civic architecture in their repeating curved rhythms, employing that most Roman of materials, concrete, from which the Colosseum in Rome and the aqueducts that conveyed water across the Roman Empire were built.

It is clear that Wright was concerned to represent the civic nature of the building in the structure, using the very latest technology and material resources to symbolize the highest traditions of civic service and pride in community. As Wright made clear, the representation of the spirit of the place and its people had to be "something commensurate with the beauty of the County." He continued "The good building is not one that

RIGHT: Promenade and translucent skylight or rooflight. In the Marin County Civic Center every office, however humble, has a view, whether to the hills and valleys of "the vista without" or of "the vista within" to the enclosed mall and gardens. The promenades that run between the buildings are also illuminated from a translucent skylight or more precisely, rooflight that floods the space with light sufficient for the growth of an extensive formal planting at ground floor level.

hurts the landscape but is one that makes the landscape more beautiful than it was before the building was built. Now in Marin County you have one of the most beautiful landscapes I have seen...I am here to help make the buildings of this county characteristic of the beauty of the county."

The spectacular site spans three hills and accommodates fairgrounds and a man-made lagoon fed from a stream flowing from the fountain sited on the cafeteria terraces. The symbolic center of the building may be regarded as the communal space of the cafeteria, which is open to employees and public alike, forming a welcoming public equivalent of Wright's "sacred hearth" in his private buildings. The complex as a whole offers both a congenial working environment and an appropriate interface for the public.

Much of the special nature of this ambience is provided by the use of glass. Top-lighting, so characteristic and continuous a feature of Wright's work is obtained by means of huge continuous skylights and a series of light wells that penetrate through three floors throughout the complex. Such light wells had been a feature of Wright's public buildings ever since he designed the Larkin Building in 1904. Used to most spectacular effect in the Johnson Wax Administrative Building light wells provided diffused natural light within an environment that eliminated views of the outside to concentrate the workforce on the task in hand. However, in the Marin County Civic Center every office, however humble, has a view, whether to the hills and valleys or of the enclosed mall and garden features.

The promenades that run between the buildings are also illuminated by means of a translucent skylight, or more precisely a roof light, that floods the space with light sufficient for the growth of an extensive formal planting at ground floor level. At third floor level, extensive views are provided through circular cut-out windows in the eaves of the roof.

ABOVE RIGHT: View up into light well. The huge complex offers both a congenial working environment and an appropriate interface for the public. Much of the ambience is decided by the imaginative and typically Wrightian use of glass. Top-lighting is provided by means of huge continuous skylights and a series of light wells that penetrate through the whole structure and also illuminate the promenades that run throughout the complex.

RIGHT: View up into one of the many light wells that penetrate through three floors throughout the complex. The promenades that run throughout the structure are roofed by a translucent skylight which diffuses the sunlight, while at third floor level extensive views of the spectacular site, which spans three hills, and the County which the building serves are provided through circular, cut-out windows in the eaves of the roof.

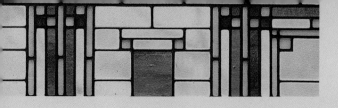

GAZETTEER

WARREN MACARTHUR HOUSE

Constructed: 1892
Address: 4852 South Kenwood, Chicago, Illinois.

The Warren MacArthur Residence was one of the twenty-five year old Wright's so called "bootleg" designs, built while Wright was apprenticed to Louis Sullivan and Jankel Adler's architectural practice. The design represents a pivotal point in Wright's use of art glass, particularly in the glass of the dining room which was almost certainly remodeled by 1902. The finest glass in the house, which employs an arrow headed design somewhat similar to that used

in the Frank Thomas House is to be found in the dining room, where the feathery arrow-head design of the upper register of the doors is repeated and elaborated upon in the sideboard fixture.

LEFT: Warren MacArthur House. Interior view of the dining room doors with sideboard beyond. Both the arrow-head design of the upper registers of the doors (which represents a radical departure in Wright's work) and the sideboard in the room beyond employ milk glass. The fine craftsmanship of Giannini and Hilgart may also be seen in the added decorative effect of the prominent balls of solder on the caming of the glass of both the doors of the room and the sideboard door glass.

FRANCIS W. LITTLE "1" HOUSE (LITTLE–CLARK HOUSE)

Constructed: 1902
Address: 1505 West Moss, Peoria, Illinois.

The first residence built by Wright for Francis W. and Mary Little consisted of a brick-built house and separate large stable. A remarkable feature is the fine art glass in the main living spaces of the house. The dining room contains ceiling fretwork grilles illuminated by electric light, a form of top-lighting first devised for his own dining room at Oak Park. In the Little House, however, the design consists of rectilinear forms with a golden tonality. It is however the glass of the entrance porch which is perhaps the most striking aspect of the entire design. The glass of the door itself employs the rectilinear forms and gold tonalities set in counterpoint against the diagonals of the glass of the arch above.

RIGHT: Interior view of the door to the entrance porch, which is somewhat reminiscent of that of the Lawrence Dana House in Springfield, if more modest in design and execution. The deep entry provides shelter for a splendid art-glass arch and entrance door which both employ the rectilinear and diagonal motifs seen elsewhere in the house and the same distinctive fall coloration.

GEORGE BARTON HOUSE

Constructed: 1903
Address: 118 Summit Avenue, Buffalo, New York.
Tours available, together with combination tour tickets for the Martin House.

Wright designed both the George Barton House and the adjacent residence for George Barton's brother in law, Darwin D. Martin. The Barton House contains fine art glass with abstract motifs drawn from nature, reminiscent of those in the Martin House but in different tonalities of green and gold, which appear to change throughout the day with the movement of light. The treatment of the windows is, however, different from any of the other Wright houses at the time. Art-glass topped side panels are used on either side of a large plate glass window, rather than in a continuous band. More familiarly, the integrated patterns of the art glass are carried through the fixtures and fittings, most notably perhaps in the splendid glass-fronted display cabinets of the dining room.

RIGHT: Detail of the living room window design seen from the exterior of the house. Abstract motifs drawn from nature, in a pattern which evokes cornstalks, are used in the upper registers of the windows, with accents of iridescent glass used to enhance the scintillating effect, interspersed with clear glass to contain the view. Similar integrated patterns are used in the glass-fronted display cabinets of the dining room.

MAMAH BORTHWICK AND EDWIN H. CHENEY RESIDENCE

Constructed: 1903
Address: 520 North East Avenue, Oak Park, IL 60302.
Private residence, currently being operated as a Bed and Breakfast.

The house is known more for the scandal that Wright incurred with its clients than for its design, although it is a particularly interesting variant on the Prairie House and contains some remarkable art glass in over fifty windows on the main floor. As with other Prairie houses of the period, the art glass designs provide a vertical emphasis to off-set the general horizontal lines of the building as a whole. The windows are particularly notable both for their glass and their elegant caming, which provide a variety of vertical emphases. Six years after the house was built, Wright, feeling that he had reached an impasse in both his career and private life was to leave his practice for Europe accompanied by Mamah Borthwick Cheney, an event that brought him great notoriety.

LEFT: View of the dining room, showing the elegance of the rectilinear design, with different windows providing a variety of linear emphasis. The tiny squares of iridiscent glass "read" in different colors from the outside, where they appear to be multi-colored, whereas against the light they appear to be simply amber and pale yellow.

DARWIN D. MARTIN HOUSE

Constructed: 1904

Address: 125 Jewett Parkway, Buffalo, NY 14214.

Open to the public, tours available in combination with a tour of the George Barton House.

The house, designed for one of Wright's most influential patrons, contains fine art glass with a series of motifs drawn from natural forms. The most distinctive of these is the "Tree of Life" design, a motif seen in the window designs, as a tripartite window, and in many of the glass fixtures and fittings. Such stylized organic tree forms have an ancient history worldwide and in terms of the

American context, so close to the heart of the Prairie House, it would seem that both the form and the symbolism of the design have parallels with the iconic American quilt.

ABOVE AND LEFT: General view of the dining room showing the dominant geometric form used in the design of the art glass throughout the house, that of the rectangle. The so-called "Tree of Life" motif may be seen in the window design and in the glass furnishings and employs both iridescent glass and milky opalescent glass in the design.

SOPHIE AND MEYER MAY RESIDENCE

Constructed: 1908
Address: 450 Madison Avenue, SE Grand
   Rapids, Michigan 49503.
Tours available.

The Sophie and Meyer May House, which was fully restored in the 1980s is particularly noteworthy for its glass designs and is typical of Wright's final Prairie House designs in that the glass ensembles, while elaborate, are an extraordinarily integrated part of the whole design, a characteristic shared with the Robie House.

The living room contains an extraordinary ensemble of art glass. The art-glass ceiling lights are rhymed with a wall of art glass windows and complemented by lamps, which are fixed to occupy a specific space as part of the whole luminous composition. The design of the ceiling light, an elegant and refined variation on a theme begun with the dining room grille of Wright's own house at Oak Park, is more complex than that of the other glass work in the space, deeper in hue and more abstract in its motifs.

ABOVE: Sophie and Meyer May Residence, Grand Rapids, Michigan. Interior of living room, showing the extraordinarily integrated ensemble of windows, skylights and lighting fixtures. The south facing living room, completed in 1910, is lit by a wall of art glass of severe geometric design, while a series of dramatic rectilinear patterned art-glass ceiling lights illuminate the room from above, an elegant and refined variation on a theme begun with the dining room grille of Wright's own house at Oak Park.

LEFT: Art glass bedroom window and glass lamp, with a set of Froebel blocks, which helped shape the child Wright's experience by teaching the basic, irreducible forms of nature that were to form such a vital part of his work. The forms of the blocks can be seen in both the lamp and the geometric design of the window. Such integrated compositions illustrate Wright's dictum "glass and light—two forms of the same thing!"

AVERY COONLEY PLAYHOUSE

Constructed: 1912
Address: 350 Fairbank Road, Riverside, Illinois.

The famous glass of the Avery Coonley playhouse (which was run as a progressive primary school) has been mostly dispersed to major museums, including the Metropolitan Museum of Art, New York, the Art Institute of Chicago, and the Victoria and Albert Museum, London, although the playhouse, which, sadly, was only used for its intended function for a few years, has been reconstructed on the original site.

The original ensemble of some three dozen windows formed a brilliant display, which Wright termed his "Kindersymphony." The balloons and confetti motifs of the design (together with the occasional stars and stripes) in which Wright draws on a quintessential American phenomenon—the parade—are exciting and celebratory in a form particularly appropriate both to the medium and to the windows' purpose in a child-centred space.

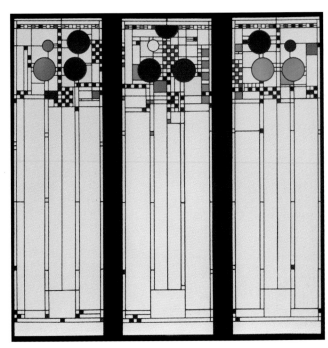

RIGHT: Avery Coonley Playhouse triptych. The windows represent a pivotal point and high-water mark in Wright's career, one in which he turned away from the use of stylized plant motifs toward an ever increasing abstraction and emphasis on pure, irreducible forms. The use of primary color, opaque geometric motifs, and fragmented, yet part-representational forms link the designs to the mainstream of contemporary avant-garde art and design in both America and Europe. The windows are valued among the icons of Modernism.

HENRY ALLEN RESIDENCE

Constructed: 1915
Address: 255 North Roosevelt Avenue, Wichita, KS 67208.
Guided tours by appointment only.

Henry Allen, who lived in the house until 1948, was governor of Kansas from 1919–23. He had presidential ambitions, thwarted when he refused the vice-presidency, which instead went to Calvin Coolidge. The house, which has undergone much restoration in recent years, is remarkable for the refinement of the design that includes much fine art glass, and for the quality of the materials used. The contractor for the house was Paul Mueller, builder of the Imperial Hotel, Tokyo, Wright's major project at the time, and a distinct Japanese influence may be perceived. The refinement of detail extended to the original range of wooden ceiling light screens which form the most striking feature of both the main living room and the dining room, as the rice paper, which concealed the electric bulbs, had a special maple leaf stencil applied.

LEFT: Interior of living room showing the double row of wooden-framed ceiling light grilles and the art-glass windows and light fixtures and fittings. The light was diffused through the fretwork grilles by means of rice paper stenciled with a special maple leaf pattern and the room is further embellished with elegant art-glass window patterns in subdued colors, repeated in the cupboard doors and the distinctly Japanese influenced light fixtures and fittings.

EDGAR J. KAUFMANN RESIDENCE "FALLINGWATER"

Constructed: 1935
Address: Bear Run (State Route 381)
Mill Run, PA.
Guided tours by reservation only.

The stream and the water cascading into it immediately beneath Fallingwater are essential elements in the design, making it the ultimate organic building, at one with its landscape setting. Glass is a crucial element in its design. The projecting, tray-like forms of the cantilevered terraces, are reached through French windows and expansive sweeps of clear glass command magnificent views of the glen beyond. As the structure of the house rests on a supportive core rather than load-bearing walls, the exterior walls could be virtually made of glass as long as they were sealed and weatherproof. Uniquely in Wright's domestic structures, the windows rise through three stories and resemble a veritable curtain of glass, that is not flat but advances in a series of stepped surfaces.

ABOVE: View from the terrace. The windows rise through three stories forming a veritable curtain of glass, integral to the character of the house as a whole. The panes are linked together in a series of steel frames. Whether they are fixed or open as doors or for ventilation, all are painted red, the color of the earth which, by this time, had become almost a signature for Wright.

LEFT: View of the living room. The major living space of some 1,800 square feet has windows on three sides. The flexibility of the space is emphasized by the fact that the corners of the room are not marked and the glass is sometimes butted directly into the stone walls.

PAUL R. AND JEAN HANNA RESIDENCE "HONEYCOMB HOUSE"

Constructed: 1936
Address: 737 Frenchman's Road, Stanford, California.
Tours offered by reservation three times a month, generally booked three months in advance.

The Hanna House marks a radical departure in Wright's work, as it is fashioned on the hexagon, giving the structure its popular name "the Honeycomb House." The use of the hexagon enabled greater flexibility in the design, allowing greater unity of exterior and interior spaces and conversion of the spaces to the changing needs of family life. As in other Usonian houses, the organic unity of the design and its site is enhanced by the use of extensively glazed window walls onto the terrace and the splendid garden beyond. The house and its terraces are integrated in quintessential Wright fashion to the contours of the hill, while the windows that command a fine view have a linking rectangular design of simple mullions that form interesting and dramatic shadows in the bright sunlight.

RIGHT: Exterior view of the Hanna House showing the extensive range of windows and the horizontal emphasis of the house, reinforced by the bands of window mullions that exactly mirror the wooden board siding that is so marked a feature of the house, both on the exterior and the interior. The fine oak tree is an essential element of the picturesque setting.

TALIESIN WEST

Constructed: 1937
Address: 12621 N. Frank Lloyd Wright Boulevard, Scottsdale, AZ 85261-4430.
A broad range of tours are available.

Taliesin West was built as the winter home and headquarters of the Taliesin Fellowship. The desert site took three years to find and, as with the original Taliesin the structure gradually evolved to accommodate the changing needs of the Fellowship. Built of hand selected "desert rubble stone," the tent-like roofing structures of the original buildings were replaced with more weatherproof materials, which still allowed the diffusion of light of the original canvas. Most significant of all is the fact that glass, which had been excluded from the early buildings began to be used in ever-increasing quantities from 1945 onward in such areas as the main drafting room and the garden room. Both spaces demonstrate the use of glass to open up spectacular vistas of the surrounding desert.

RIGHT: Interior view of the drafting room. The key motif of Taliesin West is the triangle, drawn from the nature of the site itself and its surrounding mountain ranges. Several areas are without solid walls—the mass and weight of the desert rubble stone is in strict contrast to the glazed areas. The translucent wall of the drafting room filters the light, and the spectacular "vista without" from the many windows is a stimulus to the creative imagination of those who work there.

POPE-LEIGHEY HOUSE

Constructed: 1939
Address: Woodlawn Plantation, 9000
    Richmond Highway (US 1 & Route 235)
    Alexandria, VA.
Tours available.

The house, of wood, brick, and glass mounted on a concrete pad was built to such a flexible and efficient design that the whole structure could be removed and rebuilt on its present site when threatened by a planned interstate highway. As with other Usonian houses cut-out wooden light screens are used to form an integral part of the design. Clerestory windows are formed of horizontal fretwork cut-outs which frame changing views of the

surrounding trees. The same cut-out motifs are used singly or in pairs vertically to form perforated panels in the same striking tones of Cherokee red joinery used throughout the building, creating a simple yet highly effective organic whole.

ABOVE: Interior view showing the distinctive fretwork designs of the cut out light screens used throughout the house as a unifying feature. Where the identical designs are used in such elements as the clerestory windows of the main living areas, the panels are used horizontally, here they are used vertically in pairs to off-set the horizontal emphasis seen elsewhere in the design.

LEFT: View of the main living area towards the hearth. The horizontal fretwork cut-out motifs of the clerestory windows filter the light and provide a series of continuous frames at ceiling level through which to view the trees of the surrounding plantation.

SIDNEY BAZETT (BAZETT–FRANK) HOUSE

Constructed: 1939
Address: 101 Reservoir Road, Hillsborough, California 94010.

The Bazett House was constructed on a hexagonal module, as at the first house designed by Wright in California, the Hanna House. Of relatively modest size, the Bazett House is a variant on the Usonian principle, built in the characteristic format. Wright was later asked to enlarge the design, which in its original form was less than 1,500 square feet to accommodate the Bazett's growing family. The house is a compact variant on the Usonian principle, while the

living room is designed to command views of the valley and bay in the distance. The focal point of the "vista within" of the living room is the brick built hearth, while the "vista without" is surveyed through an angled glass curtain wall and the further light is diffused into the room through a series of clerestory windows in a unique design formed of fretwork redwood batten.

ABOVE: View of the living room to the terrace beyond, showing the glass curtain wall formed of angled floor-to-ceiling windows, the most striking feature of the compact Usonian design which is based on a hexagon module. Further light is diffused into the room through a series of clerestory windows in a unique design formed of fretwork redwood batten.

STANLEY ROSENBAUM RESIDENCE

Constructed: 1939

Address: 601 Riverview Drive, Florence, AL 35630.

The house is under renovation at the time of writing and is not open to the public except by special appointment. It will be opened in 2002.

In plan, the Rosenbaum House is a variant on the basic Usonian principle, that of an "L" shape that is protected on the public side and open on to the landscape with large glazed areas on the family side of the house. As with the other Usonian houses there is a strong sense of

horizonality, a feeling enhanced by the distinctive patterns of the fretwork clerestory windows on the closed side of the house, and in the Rosenbaum residence by the use of fine cypress paneling and brick. The distinctive pierced panel design of the clerestory windows is repeated in the continuous run of illuminated light screens set into the boards of the ceiling.

ABOVE: View of the living area with the dining area beyond. The distinctive cut-out design of the clerestory windows diffuses the light above the extensive run of glass opening on to the terrace and the "vista without." The pierced fretwork panels of the clerestory windows is repeated in the illuminated ceiling panels set to the left of the hearth and above the dining area to the right.

LOWELL AND AGNES WALTER RESIDENCE "CEDAR ROCK"

Constructed: 1948–50
Address: 2611 Quasqueton Diag.
Boulevard, Quasqueton, IA.
Tours May through October. Two evening
showings, June and October.

Wright called the Walter House his "Opus
497," an indication of the number of works he had produced up until 1945 when the design
was first completed, although because of wartime building restrictions the house, which is
constructed on part of a limestone bluff on the left bank of the Wapsipinicon River, could not
begin building until 1948. The design derives from the early design from *The Ladies' Home
Journal* of "the glass house," and is remarkable for its use of glass, especially in the 900 square
foot living room. Here, in what the original plan terms "the garden room," may be seen
Wright's response to the spectacular site. To the huge main windows, Wright added a pierced
roof and clerestory windows, so that the room is flooded with enough light to sustain an
interior garden.

ABOVE: View of the garden room from the exterior. The
house is constructed from glass, steel, brick, and walnut,
with a concrete roof, that continues into a trellis with an
area of terrace beyond the screen of floor to ceiling plate
glass windows and further planting to enhance the
dominant feature of the house, the garden room.

LEFT: View of the interior of the garden room, the major
living room space of the house which measures some
900 square feet. Spectacular views of the Wapsinicon
River are commanded by the huge windows, and the
pierced roof, which contains a trellis in its overhang, and
clerestory windows, flood the room with enough light to
sustain an interior garden.

LUCILLE AND
ISADORE J. ZIMMERMAN HOUSE

Constructed: 1950

Address: 201 Myrtle Way, Manchester,
New Hampshire 03104.
Tours of house from the Currier Gallery of Art,
192 Orange Street, Manchester, NH.

Dr. Zimmerman and his wife wanted this
Usonian design to express their lifestyle,
central to which was their love of music and its
performance. Consequently the house is
designed around the main living area, which
also doubled as a concert space. The use of
glass at the site does much to compensate for the relatively modest
size of the house and is unique in Wright's work. The windows are
set high on the brick base of the building and have a distinctive keyhole motif. In the garden room, the main living area, this range of
windows is contrasted with the facing range of four square window
bays between brick piers that give directly on to the terrace and the
surrounding landscape.

ABOVE RIGHT AND INSET: Exterior view of the Zimmerman
House showing the distinctive design of the keyhole windows, which
are set high on the brick base of the building. Privacy is ensured to
the street elevation by this series of small windows formed of
perforated concrete blocks, a feature reminiscent of the California
textile block houses, thirty years before. Thus the building is made
integral to its site while ensuring its clients' well-being.

RIGHT: View of the living room interior of the Isidore J. Zimmerman
House. The distinctive range of keyhole windows is contrasted with
the facing range of large square windows giving directly on to the
terrace. The dissolution of the barrier between "the vista within" and
"the vista without" is enhanced by the fact that the lower pane of fixed
glass gives on to a continuous length of planting boxes, a feature
mirrored on the terrace side.

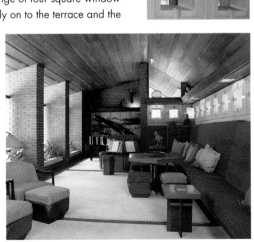

UNITARIAN MEETING HOUSE

Completed: 1951
Address: 900 University Bay Drive,
   Madison, Wisconsin 53705.
Guided tours available.

Completed when Wright was eighty-four, the distinctive triangular plan of the building had a personal meaning to the architect "I tried to build a building here that expressed that overall sense of unity...out of this triangulation you got the expression of reverence without recourse to the steeple." The distinctive triangular shape of the main auditorium gives the building impressive height, evoking the prow of a ship, or hands raised in prayer. The window wall of the prow is triangular shape and the clear glass panes originally commanded fine views of the surrounding university farmland and Lake Mendota. Light is diffused into the church through a complex system of light baffles that illuminate the rostrum and appear as a distinctive series of glazing bars on the exterior, beneath the sheltering gable.

ABOVE: View of the interior showing the construction of oak and local limestone of a type similar to that used at Taliesin, some thirty miles away. Light is diffused into the church through a complex system of light baffles that illuminate the rostrum and appear as a distinctive series of glazing bars on the exterior. Wright explained that the church was "a tangible express of what the Unitarian faith meant...And that is the unity of all things."

RIGHT: View of the exterior of the church, showing the distinctive triangular shape of the main auditorium, which evokes the prow of a ship or hands raised in prayer, and the clear glass panes and glazing bars which flood the interior with light.

FLORIDA SOUTHERN COLLEGE

Completed: 1954
Address: 111 Lake Hollingworth Drive, Lakeland, FL 33801-5698.
Self-guided walking tours are available from Visitor's Center. Call for guided tour times. Visitors
are asked to report to the Administration Building.

Florida Southern College was the most comprehensive series of buildings of Wright's career and
was in the process of building over a twenty year period, interrupted by the outbreak of the
Second World War, remaining unfinished on Wright's death. The two linked chapels, which
form the central feature of the huge complex and the Library were completed to Wright's design
and it is here that the most characteristic use of glass is found. The Pfeiffer Chapel, which has
seating for 1,000 people, is dominated by a tall glazed open tower, at ground floor level;
perforated concrete blocks are filled with small highlights of stained glass while the Danforth
Chapel contains the
most spectacular use
of stained glass.

RIGHT: Interior of the Danforth Chapel
showing the most striking use of stained glass
in the entire huge complex which was
designed by Wright and completed after his
death. The distinctive floor to ceiling red and
yellow panels of stained glass form simple
bands of primary color and are set against
alternating bands of clear glass through
which the changing skies can be glimpsed.

DONALD AND VIRGINIA LOVNESS HOUSE (1955)

Constructed: 1955
Address: 83 North, Stillwater, Minnesota.

The house is designed on a simple four-foot module, and was built by the owners to Wright's designs as a stone structure, although Wright's original design had been devised as a typical Usonian building. One of the fundamental principles of the Usonian House was affordability. Space and money were at a premium in most Usonian designs: although each house was of a generic type, such integral details as the fenestration design were unique to each house. Set on a hill near a lake, the Lovness House commands fine views from floor to ceiling windows, which are mitered at the corners. In addition to these extensively glazed areas, the clerestory windows are formed from the square module that defines and integrates the entire design, a typical feature of Wright's Usonian principle which was to give flexibility in the use of living space "breaking the box" in still more radical ways. This square motif is repeated in the lighting throughout the house, from the recessed downlights to the wooden light fixtures.

LEFT: Interior view of the main living area, showing the floor to ceiling windows, with the square module that defines the entire design being used in both the clerestory windows and the downlights that form an unbroken sequence above the windows.

BETH SHOLOM SYNAGOGUE

Completed: 1959

Address: Old York Road at Foxcroft, Elkins Park, PA 19027.

The synagogue is open Monday-Wednesday and Sunday if no activities scheduled.

Beth Sholom Synagogue is one of five religious structures designed by Wright in the final years of his life. The building is conceived as a huge, translucent, pyramid-like form, completely free of internal support and roofed translucently—Wright made reference to the structure as "a lighted mountain." The glass is protected by corrugated plastic sheeting, which gives the effect of glowing translucent blue in the sunlight, while at night the structure is brilliantly illuminated.

The softly diffused light is contrasted to the central "wings" feature of brilliantly illuminated stained glass in resonant symbolic colors in which the triangular forms repeat the basic triangle of the design module that informs the whole structure, from the ground plan itself to the integrated ornament.

ABOVE: Beth Sholom Synagogue, Elkins Park, Pennsylvania. View of the interior showing natural light flooding through the huge, translucent, pyramid-like form, which is suspended from a steel tripod weighing 160 tons, supporting the translucent glass screens that diffuse the light. Brilliantly illuminated stained glass in resonant, symbolic colors forms the central "wings" feature in which the triangular forms of the glass echo the basic triangle of the design module that informs the whole structure.

INDEX